Hey, I'm Maisie.

And I am autistic

Hey, I'm Maisie! And I am autistic

All rights reserved; no part of this publication may be reproduced or transmitted by any means, electronic, mechanical, photocopying or otherwise, without the prior permission of the publisher.

Independently published by Alison Handley

Written by Alison Handley

Illustrations and book design by
Glen Holman (www.glenholman.com)

ISBN: 9798615681257

Copyright © 2020
The moral right of the author has been asserted.
A CIP catalogue record of this book is available from the British Library

Hey, I'm Maisie!

And I am autistic

With special thanks to all the real-life Maisies
who inspired and helped to shape this book

by Alison Handley
Illustrated by Glen Holman

Hey, I'm Maisie!

I have bluey green eyes and brown wavy hair.

I'm not the tallest girl in my class – but I'm not the smallest either.

I have freckles across my nose and a beauty spot on my bottom.

And I am autistic.

Some people think that autism is only for boys. They're WRONG!

MORE and more girls are being diagnosed with autism, some when they are young and some when they are much older, as teenagers or even as adults.

I have had autism since I was born although I didn't always realise it.

Some people prefer to say someone 'has autism' or is 'on the autism spectrum'.

But saying I AM AUTISTIC is just fine for me.

No-one knows what causes autism and it isn't something that you grow out of.

When I first found out I had autism, I didn't really want to talk about it. I felt ANXIOUS and confused because I didn't really understand what it meant.

I thought it meant I was different to everybody else, and I didn't want to feel DIFFERENT.

I thought I meant there was something WRONG with me.

I thought it meant I wasn't just Maisie any more but AUTISTIC MAISIE.

I wanted my autism to GO AWAY. But I knew it wouldn't.

And that made me feel a bit SAD.

But after a while, I wanted to find out more about autism and what it meant for me.

I had lots of questions and talking to my family and friends helped me to feel much better.

People can help by... understanding I am autistic and using the words I use. And helping me to think through what that means for me and the people around me in my own time.

Now I know that being autistic is what makes me 'ME'.

I DON'T want people to say they're sorry I have autism. I'M not!

I DON'T want people to tell me I don't LOOK autistic. Just because you can't see something doesn't mean it isn't there.

I DO want people to talk to me and ask me questions about my autism.

That way, I can help them to UNDERSTAND me better.

There's a saying: If you've met one person with autism, you've met ONE person with autism.

It means we're NOT ALL THE SAME!

And sometimes girls with autism can feel and act differently to boys with autism, although that's not always the case.

That's why it's important to treat everyone with autism as an INDIVIDUAL.

These days, a lot of people are AWARE of autism, which is a GOOD THING.

But not many people REALLY KNOW what it's like to live with autism EVERY DAY, like I do.

In this book, I am going to talk about some of things I find DIFFICULT because of my autism, and some of the REALLY COOL things I have discovered about seeing and experiencing the world in a DIFFERENT way.

People can help by... asking me about my autism and taking the time to learn more about ME.

I love SCHOOL!

I have loads of favourite subjects, including art, maths and SCIENCE. I also love SINGING in the school choir.

But sometimes school can be difficult for me.

The playground is big and NOISY with lots of children running and SHOUTING, and that makes me feel ANXIOUS.

The corridors are CROWDED and sometimes other children BUMP into me because they're in such a HURRY.

The dinner hall is BUSY and LOUD too. And some days it SMELLS so bad I don't feel like eating my lunch.

Although I enjoy learning, I find tests and EXAMS very STRESSFUL. I don't always understand how to answer the questions and I worry I will run out of TIME or do BADLY.

I feel ESPECIALLY anxious at the start of a new school year. That means getting used to a NEW teacher, a DIFFERENT classroom and maybe even a NEW school. That's a lot of CHANGE all at once.

People can help by... talking to me about things that make me feel anxious at school and helping me to prepare for big changes.

I love to LEARN because there are so many things I want to know!

Like 'Why is the sky blue?' 'What do aliens really look like? And 'Why am I the only person in my family with a beauty spot on my bottom?'

My teachers say I have a good MEMORY, a BRIGHT mind and lots of BRILLIANT IDEAS!

But learning can also be really hard.

There are so many DISTRACTIONS in the classroom that I find it hard to CONCENTRATE. It can be difficult to THINK if someone is whispering or the light is flickering on and off.

Some days I have SO MUCH to think about that my mind WANDERS.... - and I get TOLD OFF for DAY-DREAMING.

I find it easier to understand and remember things that I can SEE and DO, rather than things I am told or have to work out in my head.

I often find WRITING difficult. Sometimes my thoughts are all JUMBLED UP and I just don't know where to start.

If the teacher tells us TOO MANY things at once, my brain doesn't have time to work through or PROCESS them all, and I can end up feeling anxious and CONFUSED.

Sometimes it feels as if I am the ONLY person who doesn't know WHAT TO DO which just makes things WORSE.

At times, teachers might think I am NOT TRYING, when really I just need a bit of help to get started and show everyone what I CAN DO.

People can help by... telling me things clearly, step by step, and making sure I understand instructions. And finding different ways of teaching and learning which work for me.

ANXIETY is a really big deal for me.

LOTS of things can make me feel ANXIOUS.

Some of them are BIG – like starting a new school, trying a new activity or going somewhere for the first time.

And some of them may seem quite small to other people – like having a different teacher for the day, walking into a busy shopping centre or talking to someone I don't know. But they are BIG things to me.

I can even feel ANXIOUS about HAPPY events, such as celebrating MY BIRTHDAY or going away ON HOLIDAY. And EXCITED too!

Different girls with autism will get anxious about different things, although there are some common causes – sometimes called TRIGGERS - which I will be talking about in this book.

When I am ANXIOUS I may get: angry, FRUSTRATED, upset, sad, over-excited, LOUD, quiet, MOODY or just want to be by myself.

At times, my emotions are SO STRONG that they may seem OUT OF PROPORTION to whatever is happening to me.

While at other times, people may find it difficult to see that I am feeling anxious at all.

You can help by... remembering there are all sorts of things can that make me feel anxious and all sorts of ways anxiety can make me behave. Also, you can't always tell how anxious I am inside by how I look on the outside.

Many girls with autism notice certain smells, tastes, sights and sounds more than other people. These are called SENSORY SENSITIVITIES.

I love the smell of flowers, CHOCOLATE and the rain. Mmm!

But I HATE the smell of petrol fumes, strong cheese and oranges. And I can smell them even when other people can't!

I hate LOUD noises, such as hand driers, sirens, even teachers shouting because it REALLY hurts my ears.

I like lots of different foods but I have some FAVOURITES which I would be happy to eat ALL THE TIME - like baked beans and bananas. Weird, I know!

I prefer to keep different foods, and different tastes, separate on my plate. I hate it when they all get MIXED UP together.

And there are some foods I would never eat. Please don't EVER show me a tomato!

I don't mind brushing my hair but I hate brushing my TEETH because the TASTE of peppermint makes me feel SICK.

People can help by... letting me try ways of managing my sensory sensitivities, such as using an unflavoured toothpaste or wearing ear defenders.

I am also very sensitive to certain TEXTURES, which means the way things FEEL.

Sometimes I ask for the LABELS to be cut out of my clothes because I CAN'T STAND the way they RUB against my skin and TICKLE the back of my neck.

I don't like shirts or blouses which button right up to the neck. And I can't bear ITCHY or SCRATCHY clothes next to my SKIN.

My feet are very sensitive and I hate, hate, HATE wearing socks, especially if they have rough, ANNOYING seams.

I love to have bare feet whenever I can, even outdoors. The different textures under my toes feel so GOOD!

Although some girls with autism feel more comfortable and calm if they wear TIGHT-FITTING clothes, I prefer loose-fitting tee-shirts and hoodies, and trousers or leggings made of smooth, SOFT fabrics.

Although I am OVER sensitive to some sounds, tastes and

textures, I am UNDER sensitive to temperature, which means I don't always feel HOT and COLD in the way other people do.

I don't notice the cold and like to wear a short-sleeved tee-shirt and sandals - even in the winter!

I LOVE chilling in a big BUBBLY bath, and I don't mind if the water is very HOT, so I have to be careful not to burn myself.

People can help by... taking my sensory needs seriously and recognising just how much they affect my life.

15

I hate SURPRISES!

A lot of girls with autism like their NORMAL DAY a lot more than days when things happen which they weren't EXPECTING or DIDN'T KNOW about.

Knowing what I am going to do and being able to PLAN my day, helps me to feel much LESS ANXIOUS about it.

I like to keep some things the same EVERY DAY. This is my ROUTINE.

When it's time to get dressed, I like to put my socks on FIRST (left then right), then my trousers. I wash my face and clean my teeth BEFORE I do my hair with my BEST silver hairbrush. Even at the weekend.

I eat the SAME breakfast cereal every morning and can feel very upset if I suddenly find it has RUN OUT. Help!

I like to sit at the SAME place at the table for all my meals. I even have a FAVOURITE knife and fork!

If I think we're going swimming because it's Saturday

morning and we ALWAYS go swimming on a Saturday morning, I HATE it if I SUDDENLY find out we're going shopping instead.

That doesn't mean I can't cope with CHANGE. I just like to know when it's coming so I can think about it before it happens and BE PREPARED.

You can help by... telling me if something is going to be different and I will have to change my routine, so I have TIME to PREPARE for it.

17

It may sound as if there are a lot of TRICKY things about having autism. But there are lots of REALLY GREAT things too.

When I am really interested in something, I can concentrate on it for a VERY LONG TIME.

I can sometimes get SO interested in a subject or topic that I want to think and talk about it all the time. This is often called a SPECIAL INTEREST.

When I was younger, I knew ABSOLUTELY EVERYTHING there was to know about MERMAIDS and Disney PRINCESSES!

Now my FAVOURITE subjects are DOGS, pandas, Harry Potter and the SOLAR SYSTEM.

And I LOVE watching my favourite YouTubers and playing MINECRAFT.

I think special interests are great because if you are REALLY interested in something, it means you are constantly THINKING and LEARNING – and that's good for your BRAIN!

You can help by... asking me about my special interests and realising that knowing a lot about a favourite subject, topic or hobby can be a GOOD THING.

Some people think that if you have autism, you just want to be ALONE.

But making friends and spending time with other people is very important to me.

Even though I really want to, it can be difficult for me to get to know other girls my own age and FIT IN.

I don't always understand WHAT people mean, HOW I can get to know them better or WHY things aren't working out the way I want.

I find it difficult to read people's BODY LANGUAGE and to know if they are being SERIOUS or HAVING A LAUGH.

And I feel ANXIOUS that if I do or say the WRONG thing, people will think I am STUPID or LAUGH at me.

A lot of girls my age make and lose friends very easily and that makes me UPSET and CONFUSED. Sometimes I fall out with my friends for NO REAL REASON and when that happens, I don't always know how to make things RIGHT again.

Some of the girls in my class aren't interested in the same things as me anymore. They want to talk ALL THE TIME about make-up, fashion and BOYS! BORING!!

Sometimes, it feels as if we are from DIFFERENT PLANETS. And that can make me feel LEFT OUT and a bit LONELY.

It's easier for me make friends with girls who like doing the SAME THINGS as me, and I often enjoy hanging out with girls who are OLDER or YOUNGER than me.

People can help by... saying what they mean and meaning what they say.

I have had the same BEST FRIEND since I started school.

We like doing the SAME THINGS and we never, ever get tired or BORED of each other.

We have FUN, LAUGH lots and always know the best way to CHEER EACH OTHER UP if one of us feels sad or upset. That's what BFFs are for.

Instead of having lots of friends, I prefer to spend time with people I really GET ON with. These friendships can become very CLOSE and MEAN A LOT to me.

Being a GOOD FRIEND is very important to me which means my friends and family can always RELY on me.

I love to be HELPFUL to those around me. I especially like to help my mum and dad with little jobs around the house – especially if it involves getting very messy in the kitchen or garden. Cooking, planting and digging are all great fun!

I FEEL GOOD about myself when I have been able to help someone out. And I DON'T FORGET it when people are kind to me.

I am very HONEST - sometimes a bit too honest as I'm not very good at hiding the TRUTH and I tend to say what I think. But I don't JUDGE other people and I like things to be right and FAIR.

I also have a strong and rather CRAZY sense of HUMOUR. Just ask my best friend!

People can help by... recognising that although I sometimes struggle with friendships, I have a lot of qualities that make me a really GREAT FRIEND.

My second best friend is my DOG, Biscuit!

Many girls with autism have a SPECIAL BOND with ANIMALS, which means they love spending time with their pets.

I really enjoy visiting farms and zoos and finding out more about animals from all over the world. Especially PANDAS!

But Biscuit is my very BEST PAL and we make a really 'pAWESOME' team! Sorry!

Biscuit helps me to feel less STRESSED and ANXIOUS and I love to STROKE and CUDDLE him after a busy day at school.

It's great learning how to CARE for animals – and a whole load of FUN too!

I spend lots of time PLAYING with Biscuit and taking him for WALKS in the park. His all-time favourite game is FETCH!

Lots of people want to say 'hi' to Biscuit when we are out and about and this has helped me to feel more CONFIDENT about meeting new people.

You can help by... remembering that relationships with animals and pets can be just as valuable as those with other human beings.

Some girls are good at HIDING the difficulties they have because of their autism, which is called 'MASKING'.

This is because we have learned what to do and say and how to FIT IN, by watching and copying those around us.

'Masking' doesn't mean that our autism no longer EXISTS, although it does mean that other people may find it harder to know we're finding things difficult.

Although we can be good at COPYING others and behaving in the way people EXPECT, this can also be very TIRING.

People don't always see the anxiety bubbling around INSIDE me during a NORMAL DAY.

But it can build and build until by the end of the day, it feels as if my BRAIN is about to EXPLODE!

I feel so EXHAUSTED that all I want to do is HIDE AWAY in my bedroom or snuggle down under my favourite blanket.

At times like this, I may not feel like seeing or talking to anyone. Instead, I prefer to listen to my favourite MUSIC, play my favourite COMPUTER GAMES or READ my favourite books for a while, in my own space.

This helps me to RECHARGE my batteries – or get my ENERGY LEVELS back up – and feel ready for the next day.

If I have had a particularly stressful day, this can take a long time, even several HOURS.

You can help by... understanding that even though I may be good at 'masking' my anxieties, I still need help dealing with them. Giving me the time I need to relax in my own space and in my own way is very important.

Many girls with autism will experience MELTDOWNS.

These happen when a situation is so OVERWHLEMING that someone loses control of their behaviour for a short period of time.

They are NOT the same as temper tantrums although if someone is shouting or crying because of a meltdown, or even hitting out, it can look similar.

Lots of different things can trigger a meltdown, including SENSORY sensitivities, a CHANGE in routine and ANXIETY, which may have been BUILDING UP during a stressful day.

A lot of these things can be very difficult for someone else to see so they may not realise how I am feeling.

When I start to feel anxious, there are a number of things I have learned to do to help myself feel CALMER, including listening to MUSIC, SQUEEZING a stress ball and using FIDDLE TOYS.

But although these can be very helpful, they can't always stop my brain from becoming so OVERLOADED that I have a meltdown.

Afterwards, I usually CRY a lot and feel VERY SAD for a while.

It helps if people around me STAY CALM and let me recover in my own time and in my own SAFE SPACE.

Sometimes, I like to TALK later about what happened with someone I trust, but not always.

People can help by... understanding the difference between a 'temper tantrum' and a meltdown. Giving me time and space to recover and allowing me to talk things through if I want to, really helps.

If I set my mind to something, I can achieve REALLY AMAZING things.

I am not easily distracted or put off, even if someone tells me my idea is NO GOOD or it WON'T WORK.

I can be very PERSISTENT and am more likely to SEE THINGS THROUGH right to the end, than to give up when things get tough.

Perhaps that's because I am more interested in ACHIEVING my own GOALS, than in competing with other people.

I am very CREATIVE and people who know me say I have such a fantastic IMAGINATION that I often SURPRISE and AMAZE them.

I am good at 'thinking outside the box' which basically means looking at things in a different way to other people.

That means that I may be able to come up with a NEW IDEA or a find a NEW SOLUTION to a problem which other people haven't thought of.

You can help by... remembering that being able to think and see things differently can be a real STRENGTH.

I love to talk and people would describe me as a bit of a CHATTERBOX.

But everyday conversations can be rather CONFUSING to me at times.

I may take it LITERALLY if someone uses a word or phrase I don't know, and I find it hard to 'read between the lines' and work out the HIDDEN meanings behind things I read or hear.

I find some EXPRESSIONS really difficult to understand. If someone thinks I have got a lot of energy, why do they say I am 'full of beans'?!

I love to LAUGH and I have a great SENSE OF HUMOUR. But I don't always 'get' JOKES which other people find funny and I may not realise when someone is being SARCASTIC.

It can be difficult for me to understand what people are saying by the LOOK on their faces or the TONE of their voices too.

It is much easier for me if people SPEAK CLEARLY and say exactly WHAT THEY MEAN.

Sometimes, having something to look at, such as pictures and photographs, drawings or symbols, can also be really helpful. These are called VISUAL SUPPORTS.

I often need a bit of extra time to PROCESS information and it helps if I am not told lots of things AT ONCE.

Asking me TOO MANY questions, and putting PRESSURE on me to answer QUICKLY, can be OVERWHELMING.

You can help by... remembering that if I don't answer you straight away, I may still be processing what you have said. Please give me a bit of time and don't confuse me by talking even more!

My family and friends would describe me as KIND, loving and CARING.

Some people think that people with autism can't share other people's feelings and don't understand emotions.

But that's not true.

I don't always show my EMOTIONS in the way you might expect. I sometimes laugh when I am shocked or scared, for example. I don't know why, it just happens.

But I DO feel emotions VERY DEEPLY and this can be hard sometimes.

If someone says something which UPSETS me, it can take me a long time to get over it. I may remember feeling hurt or let down by someone, long after everyone else has MOVED ON and forgotten all about it.

If I am worried I have said or done the wrong thing, I may go OVER AND OVER it in my head.

When I hear about children or animals who are hungry or in pain, it can make me feel VERY SAD INDEED.

But it also makes me want to do everything I can to HELP and make things BETTER, and I think that's a very GOOD THING.

While some girls with autism don't like being touched, I enjoy lots of HUGS and KISSES from those closest to me.

I am not very good at hiding my FEELINGS. Whether I am happy or sad, angry or upset, thankful or excited, you will probably know about it.

People can help by... helping me to talk through things that hurt or upset me, and remembering that even if I sometimes show my emotions in unexpected ways, I still feel them very deeply.

I have a good EYE FOR DETAIL, which means I often notice things that other people miss.

This makes me GOOD at games where you need to look CAREFULLY and very aware of the WORLD AROUND ME.

I am always ASKING QUESTIONS and trying to MAKE SENSE of the world we live in.

Perhaps I would make a good detective!

Although being very sensitive to smells, tastes, sights and sounds can be difficult at times, it also means I really appreciate NATURE, from beautiful flowers and plants to the sea and stars and even creepy crawlies! Caterpillars are COOL!

I love being OUTDOORS and find the scent of flowers, the sound of birds talking to each other and the feel of soft grass under my feet, really AMAZING!

It makes me sad that a lot of people are so BUSY getting on with their lives that they never stop to SEE AND ENJOY the world around them.

You can help by... talking to me about the world we share and seeing it through my eyes once in a while.

Despite my strengths, I sometimes feel BAD about myself.

Although I know there are a lot of really GOOD things about me and my life, I find it easy to FORGET this at times.

I am very SENSITIVE which means my feelings can get HURT very easily. If someone says something bad, I often take it PERSONALLY, even when it wasn't aimed at me.

Sometimes tiny little problems can grow bigger and BIGGER in my head until they feel like huge DISASTERS.

And when things don't go the way I planned, I am likely to BLAME myself.

Because of this, BOOSTING MY CONFIDENCE and PRAISING ME when I do something well is very important to me.

Something as simple as a 'high five' from a friend or a 'well done' from my mum or dad can make me feel MUCH BETTER about myself.

I love getting stickers, praise points and other rewards from my teachers at school. Lots of encouragement boosts my self-confidence and helps me to go on and do EVEN BETTER!

Sometimes I need reminding that when things don't go the way I want them to TODAY, there is always TOMORROW.

By trying to THINK POSITIVE and LEARN from my mistakes, I can see that I am STRONGER and more RESILIENT than I think.

You can help by... telling me when you are pleased with me or I have done something well. If I know you are proud of me, I find it easier to feel PROUD of myself.

39

Although I have some special interests, which I talked about earlier in this book, there are many other things I enjoy doing too.

Although it has taken me a bit longer to learn some skills, like riding a bike and catching a ball, I really enjoy being sporty and ACTIVE.

This helps me to feel HAPPIER, more relaxed and less ANXIOUS about things.

There is nothing I like better than to JUMP up and down on my TRAMPOLINE after a stressful day at school! BOING, boing!!

I often feel anxious about starting a new activity or trying something I haven't done before. So it helps if people are PATIENT and give me the time and space I need to feel CONFIDENT enough to HAVE A GO.

Once I've plucked up the courage, I may find I'm really good at it!

I enjoy scootering, roller skating, dancing and especially

swimming - I love the FEELING of water on my body and I really enjoy SPLASHING around!

Many of the things I like doing are similar to other girls my age. But I still enjoy some of the things I liked when I was younger, such as dressing my DOLLS, reading FAIRYTALES and MAKING THINGS out of sand, play doh and modelling clay, which FEEL great!

People can help by... recognising that I enjoy lots of different activities which meet my needs in different ways.

41

When I grow up, I would like to help GIRLS WITH AUTISM just like me.

I would tell them some of things I have LEARNED about MYSELF and MY AUTISM.

And I would LISTEN to what they had to say about their own EXPERIENCES of LIVING WITH AUTISM.

I would like to ENCOURAGE and INSPIRE them by telling them that women with autism have achieved GREAT THINGS in many different fields, from science and technology to public speaking, sport, entertainment and the environment.

I would like to reassure them that autism is not something to HIDE or to be ashamed of. It's simply the WAY WE ARE.

And I would like to remind them that at a time when more and more girls and women are being diagnosed with autism, they are very definitely NOT ALONE.

Most of all, I would like to help create a world where girls and boys, men and women with autism, are UNDERSTOOD, VALUED and ACCEPTED for WHO WE ARE.

You can help by... remembering that although I have autism, I have ambitions, hopes and dreams just like anyone else.

Thank you for reading this book.

If you are a girl who has been diagnosed with autism, there will probably be some things about me that you recognise and others that you don't.

Don't forget, just because we both have autism, it doesn't mean we are THE SAME. Autism is a broad SPECTRUM and one girl's experience of autism may be different from another's.

However, there are some common CHARACTERISTICS you may RECOGNISE and which we SHARE.

I hope this book will encourage you to DISCUSS your autism with your friends and family and the people around you, and to think about those things which make us DIFFERENT and those ways in which we are ALIKE.

If you know, or are working with, a girl who has autism, remember that a diagnosis of autism is not an end but a BEGINNING, and there is so much you can do to encourage and support her.

Finally, if you think you or someone you know MAY have autism, don't be discouraged from getting the help and support you need. Remember, GIRLS CAN HAVE AUTISM too!

People can help by... remembering that although my autism is a big part of my life, there is A LOT MORE to me than my diagnosis.

At the end of the day, I am still MAISIE and I am still ME!

Printed in Great Britain
by Amazon

27740839R00030